21 Ways to Skyrocket Your Creativity

21 WAYS

to **skyrocket**
your
creativity

Tony Laidig

Discover! BOOKS™
an Imprint of Imagine! Books™

High Point, North Carolina

21 Ways™ Series, Book 5

Published by Discover! Books™
an Imprint of Imagine! Books™
PO Box 16268, High Point, NC 27261
contact@artsimagine.com

Imagine! Books™ is an enterprise of Imagine! Studios™
Visit us online at www.artsimagine.com

Copyright © 2012 Tony Laidig
Cover Design © 2012 Imagine! Studios™
Illustrations by Drawperfect, purchased at istockphoto.com

ISBN 13: 978-1-937944-07-0

First Discover! Books™ printing, May 2012

Praise for *21 Ways to Skyrocket Your Creativity*

"Whew! I thought I was a creative person (at least in my own mind...), but Tony, you've knocked it out of the park.

Watching you online has demonstrated how talented and creative you truly are. Your 21 Ways really proved to me that there are so many opportunities to be more creative that I've missed. The following were my favorite that made me think a lot more creatively:

Pattern interruption—the only difference between a grave and a rut I've been told are the dimensions. This technique helped me understand that I could create an opening for something new by moving out of my comfort zone a little bit.

Clearing—In the movie "For the Love of the Game," pitcher Kevin Costner had trained his mind to respond to his command: "Clear the mechnaism." When he said that, the crowd disappeared and he became one with the catcher and the ball. I know it was a movie, but I wanted that ability to focus. You have shown me how that actually works with Clearing.

Monotonous Activities—It's so important for me to "carry water and chop wood" because that's when my mind is not occupied with the list. And the committee that lives between my ears actually allow me to listen when I'm focused on menial details. Best ideas come in the shower they say, and now I know why.

Idea Mashing—I used to call this 'Prosperity Scrabble.' And it is amazing how it works. I love this idea mashing technique and am so happy you've included it in your book.

Tony, this is an excellent book for people to find their creativity. They can look at you and see that you're walking the walk the too!"

—David Perdew, Niche Affiliate Marketing System, Inc.
MyNams.com

"In *21 Ways to Skyrocket Your Creativity*, Tony spells out practical solutions to help you get past the excuses and distractions of daily routines and chaos. Buy this book to ignite your inspiration!"

—Nathan Martin, Publisher of *Sound Wisdom*

"Shazam! If you're looking for a boost in your creativity super powers, Tony Laidig delivers in this short, yet motivating, idea-packed book. As someone who is often accused of being creative myself, I have often used many of these ways to jump-start my own creativity; I raise my right hand and say, "Yes they work!" This is one of those books you'll want to keep nearby to reference in those moments when you're feeling stuck or looking for that one burst of creative energy that will send you careening toward massive success. I personally thanked Tony for writing it, and you will too!"

—Felicia Slattery, M.A. M.Ad. Ed., best-selling author of
21 Ways to Make Money Speaking and *Kill the Elevator Speech*

Dedication

For all you creative souls who have paintings yet to paint, music to write, photographs to capture, books to pen, dances to express, inventions to create, solutions to offer, and every other creative form waiting to take flight from within you...

this book is for you!

Acknowledgements

Over the course of my life, there have been people who called me a dreamer, said I always had my head in the clouds, taught me never to question and encouraged me to play it safe.

There were also those who challenged me to question everything, take risks, ignore "because I said so" and convinced me that I could do anything I could dream or imagine. I'm grateful to all of them because they not only defined where the boundaries were, but also showed me how to cross them into a playground of limitless possibility.

To my Mom and Dad, Rosalee and Veryl Laidig: You provided me with the encouragement and tools to keep my creativity alive at an early age. I'm so grateful for that.

To my daughters, Ashlea and Courtney: You represent and reflect a living creative expression that is always growing, ever-changing and keeps me guessing. Please never stop... grin.

I'm also indebted to Betty Eisaman, Arthur Houck, Don Nori, Sr. and other mentors who challenged me to "play" at a much higher level.

I would also like to thank my good friend and publisher, Kristen Eckstein, for giving me the opportunity to share my ramblings with others. I appreciate the "21 Ways" platform because its quick shots of business and creative "energy" enrich and enhance our businesses without all the fluff and embellishment so common today.

Lastly, I would like to acknowledge all the bizarre, strange and unexplainable experiences I've had over the years. While I may not have understood the "why" or "what" at times, you certainly have kept my life interesting.

Introduction

You are a creator! It's what you were born to do. It's how you are wired. Unfortunately, life often gets in the way of your creative process and you fall haplessly into a predictable routine of status quo. You wake up, maybe eat breakfast if you're lucky, drive to work, do your job, drive home, eat dinner, and fritter away your evening watching TV or catching up on Facebook.

Deep down, you want more. There's something within you that's screaming to be expressed, but you've rehearsed all the reasons why you can't be creative so many times that the objections seldom arise now.

✓ There's no time

✓ I don't have the money

✓ I'm not very creative

✓ My creations aren't that great

✓ I'm no Michelangelo

✓ Who would buy what I make, anyway?

On and on go the excuses.

Perhaps you're one of the lucky ones. Perhaps you've chosen to make the creative process a priority in your life. Whether for business or recreation, you understand the need and benefit of embracing your creativity within. But there are times when you feel that you've hit a wall. You're facing a moment when you *need* to be creative and the inspiration isn't coming. What do you do? How do you "create" the breakthrough you need to allow your creativity to begin flowing again?

This book is for people in both camps, which probably includes you. The "21 Ways" included within these pages fall primarily into two categories: *Perspective* and *Flow*. I have found that a simple shift in perspective or the elimination of "blockages" can plug you into all the creativity you desire.

Before we dig in, let's establish a core definition for creativity. *Creativity* is simply taking something that forms within you, an idea, and giving it an outward expression. Creativity is a means to an end. It's the key that starts the engine, so let's get started!

Tony Laidig

WAY 1

Pattern Interruptions

Let's face it: We are, by and large, creatures of habit. Beginning at birth, our social standing, race, culture, upbringing, and religious practices define our identity. As a result, much of what you do and believe about yourself, business, success, or failure is based upon habits of thinking, habits of belief, and your corresponding actions. Often, these habits are so much a part of our everyday existence that we are completely unaware of them, much as fish are unaware of the water they swim in.

There is a legend told of the arrival of the explorer's ships in the New World. To the inhabitants of the islands, the ships were completely invisible because they had no frame of reference to process what they were witnessing. Their habits and programming did not include massive sailing vessels. But then something interesting occurred. A local medicine man was standing on the beach and noticed variations in the waves but didn't know what was causing them. After a period of time, however, he became aware of the ships and he was able to see them. What happened? A pattern interruption (the variations in the waves) led him into a new way of seeing.

Pattern interruptions simply help break us out of our habits and tap into the creative process in new ways that were previously invisible to us. A pattern interruption can be anything as long as it interrupts the patterns or habits that result from our programming. A pattern interruption could be something as simple as driving a different way to work; walking your dog in a new area; trying something you've never tried before, such as skydiving; or, my own personal favorite, driving fast sports cars.

Breaking up those habitual, everyday patterns opens up the possibility for new ways of thinking. It can also present us with inspiration that only would have come through the experience of our pattern interruption. Einstein is credited with a definition of insanity: doing the same thing over and over and expect a different result. Our habits are like that, hence the need to "interrupt" our routine.

Questions also serve as excellent tools to create pattern interruptions in our routine. I no doubt added many gray hairs to my mother's head because I always challenged everything. I always asked why.

Why do I have to do it *this* way? Who says *that* way is the best or correct way? What if I tried it like *this*? What would happen if ... ?

I want to challenge you the same way. If you're feeling "stuck" or in a rut, why not interrupt your routine with something new or different? Simple changes to our otherwise mundane existence can result in a massive insight or creative breakthrough that can result in a greater level of success in your life and business. But *only* if you "interrupt the regularly scheduled programming."

2

Music

Music can have a huge impact on your creative process because of its limitless forms of expression, meaning, and interpretation. It moves us in ways that little else can and affects us emotionally, spiritually, even physiologically. Certain rhythms and keys cause measureable responses that, when used deliberately, can cause us to become more at ease, relaxed, inspired, and yes, more creative. It's one of the reasons why casinos tune all the bells and buzzers to the key of C. This musical key has been shown to make people the most "happy" (the key of D minor, by the way, is considered the "saddest" key). Happy people are more likely to spend more time in the casino and feel bolder about gambling.

You've likely also heard of the "Mozart effect," where research has shown that musical pieces, such as those composed by Mozart, can cause creativity to soar. The Mozart effect has also been credited with other benefits as well, including improved test scores, accelerated healing of the body, and a calming effect with children.

As a graphic designer, I often used music to inspire and direct my creativity. One project I designed was a graphic novel about children and the different abuses they suffer. In the book, I had to visually portray different types of abuses that children go through to complement the poems and the stories that were collected in the book. At first I struggled with the designs because I honestly didn't know how to tap into that level of creativity since I had never experienced abuse. But then, the idea came to me to use music to direct my creativity.

At the time, there was a band out, called Circle of Dust, who played a lot of dark, techno-industrial music. The founder of the band went on to create much of the music used in Chris Angel's television program, *Mind Freak*. I spent three days listening to nothing but this dark music, and it took me creatively to the place where I was able to create the types of images I needed for the project. Music has that ability.

The power that music wields over us offers a very effective vehicle for plugging into creative innovation. Its ability to transport us to another state of awareness is unparalleled and, when used deliberately, can ramp up your creativity like nothing else. Try this. Listen to different kinds of music, especially styles you don't normally listen to or even like. Observe how the music makes you feel. How do you respond to jazz versus club music, to blues versus heavy metal? And for goodness sake, if you've always listened to the same types of music your entire life, try something new and break the pattern (see Way 1: Pattern Interruptions).

WAY 3

Clearing

I want you to picture the drainpipe attached to your bathtub. Over the course of time, hair, little pieces of soap, and Lord knows what else slowly begin to clog the pipe, until one day you notice that the water doesn't flow quite as well as it used to. Why? Because of all this crud that has built up in the pipe. The only way to get the water flowing freely again is to clear the clog. The same thing happens to us!

Just as our bathroom drains can get clogged with crud, so too can our creative flow get clogged. Negative emotions, bitterness, unforgiveness, fear, and self-doubt are just of few of the clogging mechanisms that sometimes need to be cleared in order to release your creative flow once again.

In my own experience, I have seen where my own negative emotion has stopped the flow of sales into my business. My business was bottoming out and I couldn't figure out why it was happening. Then a conversation with a mentor led to a major breakthrough in a very unexpected way. Something was indeed clogging my creative flow, but it wasn't something I expected.

For years I struggled with some major anger issues and an ongoing sense of loss. I feared that every time I gained success or something good in my life, something would happen to steal it away from me. Ever felt that way?

During the conversation with my mentor, a sudden flash of memory took me back to my great grandmother. I was the love of her life and I thought she was the greatest person in the world. When I was 8 years old, she passed away from a brain aneurism. Because of my age, my parents were reluctant to tell me right away that she had died. It was nearly two weeks before they told me.

As an 8-year-old, I didn't know how to emotionally process her loss and, as a result, I buried those emotions. Over the years, those unresolved emotions festered into anger, resentment and fear of loss. When I finally discovered the emotional clog that resulted, I was able to release it and something changed within me. Once I released this blockage in my heart, the change was immediate. The flow of creativity increased exponentially and my business sales jumped by a factor of three in just weeks.

Clearing emotional clogs doesn't have to be a difficult process. It requires honesty and a willingness to do whatever it takes to make "it" right. Chances are that an event has come to mind while you've read this. So here is what I want you to do—make it right. Do what it takes to move beyond the issue. If it involves a person who is no longer living, forgive yourself and release the emotion for good. You will be blown away with the result. I could share dozens of stories from my own life how this one method—clearing—led to amazing success and breakthrough in my creativity. It will for yours as well.

WAY 4

Monotonous Activities

Did you ever notice how some of your best ideas come to you when you're doing mundane, monotonous things? How many times have you gotten a great idea in the shower? It's hard to imagine that boring activities such as taking a shower, driving your car, or going for a walk could lead to breakthrough creativity, but that's often the case! These activities require very little thought and can be accomplished, at times, almost on autopilot.

I'm one of those people who enjoy standing in a hot shower and just allowing the water to run over me... no thoughts, no expectations, just warm, running water. I've found that some of my most creative ideas come from those times. I also pace... a *lot*. Every night I spend time, usually an hour or more, walking around my house or around the neighborhood, just thinking, processing, questioning. This daily practice has led to some amazing breakthroughs in my personal life and in my business.

Why does it work? Why does it appear that many people, perhaps even you, experience great insights and creativity while doing the most mundane of tasks? Often in those situations, the normal stimuli we are inundated with during the day are gone. With all the outside "noise" gone, our subconscious can actually get through to us much more easily. Our subconscious is always broadcasting messages, but we often miss them because of all the other noise and chatter that distract us. During monotonous activities, the tables are turned and we can hear that "still, small voice."

Creativity says, "Finally, I can get a word in edgewise! Finally I can show you a thing or two!" The biggest challenge we face in these situations is making sure the ideas that come to us are captured. I've found that it can be extremely easy to forget those "life-changing" ideas from those times because I'm so relaxed. We think, "This is the most incredible idea I've ever received; there is no way I'm going to forget it!" We finish showering, dry off, go into the bedroom, and it's gone, just that quickly.

Get in the practice of having a journal or digital audio recorder with you at all times. Not in the shower, of course, but have a recording device of some sort available as soon as you finish. (Or get some Crayola® Bathtub Crayons to write on the walls before you forget that great idea.) I've learned from experience to keep notepads everywhere. I have them in every room of my house, in both cars, everywhere. It's a good practice to follow and you'll find you more readily record your thoughts that way.

Now, to take this creativity booster method one step further, why not PLAN for regular, monotonous activities in your life to increase your creativity in a predictable way? No, I'm not telling you to shower more, but I am saying you can be more deliberate in your creative efforts. Nothing beats walking around a quiet house at night with no agenda except to listen. And, for the record,

I walk or pace because I know that the moment I sit down, sleep will follow shortly. If you want creativity to flow, you have to be awake to realize that it is.

Resources in this Way:

 Crayola® Bathtub Crayons

5

Brainstorming

Brainstorming can serve as a powerful creativity booster because it moves you beyond yourself to synergistically benefit from the insights and genius of others. Many times we can develop tunnel vision in a creative situation and, at times, miss even obvious solutions because we are too close to the problem. Add a few more perspectives, however, by adding like-minded friends, peers, or mentors into the mix, and creative breakthrough often ensues.

In his legendary book, *Think and Grow Rich*, Napoleon Hill shares the power and importance of mastermind groups, which are essentially structured brainstorming sessions. I've found this type of regular interaction invaluable to both my business and personal life. The truth is we each have unique perspectives that, when brought together, can lead to some pretty amazing and satisfying results.

A few years ago, I decided to try an experiment involving brainstorming and masterminds, except in a very different (and perhaps strange) way. In this experiment, I visualized a room with a conference table and chairs. Around the table sat friend and business associates, both living and dead. I had Napoleon Hill there, and my friend Pat O'Bryan was there along with other Internet marketers whom I didn't know personally. I imagined myself walking into the room, sitting down at the head of the table, and seeing each of the six or eight people there. I then posed a question to them. I asked them for creative ideas on how to best create a certain product idea I had. I told them I would leave them to it and check back the next day. I then proceeded with my work for the day.

The next day, something unexpected happened. I closed my eyes once again and visualized myself walking into the conference room, but when I walked in, what I discovered surprised me. Strewn around the table were empty pizza boxes, beers and notepads everywhere. I asked what was going on and was told that the group got hungry while working through the night (weird, I know). When I asked what ideas they came up with, the response blew me away. The answers they shared were creative and nothing like any ideas I had considered. I opened my eyes long enough to write down what was shared and then kept going back and forth between listening and writing. From that day forward I knew that I was onto a powerful creativity tool. I know it sounds a bit crazy, but the result was unmistakable; it worked!

Of course, brainstorming doesn't have to involve "imaginary friends." As a matter of fact, I encourage you to talk with those you trust in your life—men and women who will support and encourage your ideas rather than call you crazy. The result will often be exactly what you needed to hear.

WAY

6

Brain Dumping

The phrase "brain dumping" is pretty self-explanatory. Simply stated, brain dumping is the act of "dumping" or capturing every single thought you have on a given topic without qualifying or editing those thoughts. Consider the process you go through when folding your laundry. The jumble of clothes is removed from the dryer and dumped into a laundry basket. Then, one piece at a time, the clothes are sorted, folded and put away in your dresser or closet. Brain dumping works the same way.

Brain dumping is an important creativity booster for a number of reasons. First, just as a full pitcher of water cannot hold more water, your conscious mind can only hold so many thoughts. There comes a point when trying to manage and remember all the "stuff" swirling around in your head becomes challenging, and you begin to forget more than you remember. Dumping those thoughts creates a vacuum in your thought processes and allows MORE thoughts, ideas, and creativity to flow in.

The two best methods you can us to capture this download of information are to write it down or journal it or record yourself using a digital recording device of some type. Either method works well, and I have used both myself. My preferred method of brain dumping is journaling, but you should use whichever method works best for you. I have also found that choosing a private, quiet place to record your thoughts is also very conducive to remembering and recording more of your thoughts. Also, as I mentioned earlier, it is important to record your thoughts without qualifying them or editing them. Both processes can hinder the flow of ideas, hence defeating the purpose of the brain dump. Once you are finished, go back a read over your notes or listen to the audio. Only then does it make sense to organize your thoughts into a cohesive form.

As you begin to practice this on a regular basis, you will begin to discover that the flow of creativity and innovation will increase because you've made room for it. You know more than you can imagine and brain dumping "primes the pump" to enable your wealth of inner knowledge to bubble up and touch the world around you. You will soon realize that this can create a steady flow of creativity that will benefit you in every area of your life, not just your business.

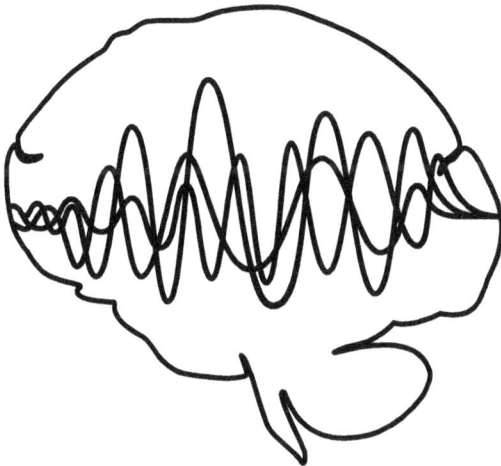

WAY 7

Immersion

Immersion is another method I frequently use to increase my creativity. Immersion can take a number of forms, but it is, essentially, surrounding yourself with a new, fully sensory experience, where your five physical senses are impacted. You are "immersed" in an environment different from your normal experience.

The most common immersive experience would be to get out into nature. Go for a walk to take in the sights, sounds, and smells. They have a way of re-programing you in a healthy way. It's been proven that sunlight affects us in a positive way physically, emotionally, and physiologically. Breathing in the fresh air (as opposed to the stale air in your office) increases blood flow and makes you more alert. The sound of rushing water or waterfalls soothes and relaxes you because rushing water represents perfect white noise by covering the full spectrum of sound.

Other immersive environments could include snorkeling, skydiving, a sweat lodge, or the opera. Yes, immersion is a form of pattern interruptions, but is also very healthy for your mental health.

I remember my first experience in a sweat lodge because it had a profound effect on me. Imagine sitting in a completely dark, enclosed environment with eleven other people. In the middle of the lodge were super-heated rocks. The sweat leader, a Cherokee elder, was chanting and pouring water over the hot rocks to create steam. The heat was overwhelming and I nearly panicked, because I felt as if I couldn't breathe. We took turns singing some of the old tribal songs, but all I could think about at first was, "I have to get out of here." It was definitely a battle of mind over matter. However, once I made a conscious decision to relax, assuring myself that I would be okay, I calmed down. I relaxed.

The sweat lodge represents the womb—a complete, immersive environment—and so when we emerged from the lodge after fifteen or twenty minutes of intense heart and into the bright spring day, it was like being reborn. The feeling I experienced was so exhilarating it wiped away and cleared many of the blockages in my life. The experience had a meaningful impact on my life and brought a lot of clarity. That's the power of immersion!

I'm not saying you must experience a sweat lodge in order to release your creativity. Spending time in nature can be just as powerful. What makes immersion important from a creativity perspective is that it provides a different perspective or frame of reference. It's important to be observant when in an immersive situation. Pay attention to your thoughts and emotions. Very often, the ideas and feelings that surface during those times will provide you with a key to breaking through your creative block.

Tonight, if the skies are clear, go outside away from any lights and stare up into the sky. Soak in the sights, be aware of the sounds around you, and consider your place in a vast universe. It may just be the best creativity-changing experience you've ever had!

8

Culture Shifting

"Culture Shifting" is a phrase I coined to refer to the process of viewing our experiences from worldviews other than our own. We have a tendency, especially in America, to think that everyone sees things the same way we do. Of course, nothing could be further from the truth. Culture (and all that defines it) plays a profound role in how we view the world around us, in ways you may have never considered before.

I first became aware of this idea when I was studying linguistics. I was comparing the differences of worldview based on language and place. Thanks to excellent research presented by Benjamin Whorf (*Language, Thought, and Reality*) and others, I realized that the world of creativity was much bigger than I had imagined.

We have a tendency in Western culture to think from the perspective of noun-verb-noun. For example, when see a horse in a field, we might say, "The horse is in the field"—noun, verb, noun. To some indigenous tribes however (the Hopi would be an example), their view of the horse in the field would be completely different because their language is verb-based, not noun-based. As a result, when they see a horse in a field, they view it as an active, changing experience, not just an observation. They see the "horse" as having a "horse experience." It's alive and changing. The same is true with the field. The field is alive and active; it's a field experience. Their language acknowledges that the grass is growing, bugs are crawling, dead leaves are decomposing. The field is active, and the horse's presence is affecting the field. Everything is alive and connected. Somehow, their verb-based words convey that alive-ness, where, in Western culture, we objectify everything.

Viewing the world around you from this new verb-based perspective (culture shifting) gives a whole new spin on how you do things and interact with the world around you, especially from the perspective of business. Consider your business as a verb. You want your business to be active, moving, flowing, vibrant, energetic, and alive. Take the perspective that it's actively connected to everything else. Quantum physics is beginning to prove that is everything truly is connected. Everything you do in business is connected and related to everything else you do, so your business and products are very active things.

Whenever you create a product or offer a service, you're not just creating a product (an object). You are setting things in motion because that product or service has the potential of changing people's lives. It has the potential of sparking something in your customer that gives that person an idea that leads to success.

Another fun example of how culture shifting can work is through the use of W.W.J.D., What Would Jesus Do. I'm sure you've seen products with that question on it. I use a variation of that in my business to shift my creativity. I might ask myself, "What would Donald Trump do in this situation? How would he respond?" I've even taken this exercise as a far as imagining that I was sitting across the table from an Internet marketer whom I knew of, but didn't know personally. In my mind, I asked him, "Is there something in my business that I'm overlooking? What am I missing?" One response I received from this scenario resulted in a product I created that netted me nearly $100,000. Before the exercise, I hadn't even considered the idea. So it was a huge (and profitable) shift!

Puzzles

Puzzles are one of my personal favorite ways to boost creativity. Conventional wisdom says that the creative process is primarily a "right-brain" activity, but I've found that spending time doing left-brain tasks, such as analytical and logical thinking or problem solving, can enhance creativity. Think about it, puzzles are, in and of themselves, very creative in their design. Yet, the solutions often require logical and critical thinking. There are often patterns to puzzles or distinct methodic solutions that require keen observation. These same types of thinking can be applied to the creative process as well.

There are many types of puzzles that may appeal to you and help bring breakthrough to your creative process. I few types of puzzles I have used to boost my creativity:

- ✓ Crossword puzzles

- ✓ Sudoku

- ✓ Sherlock Holmes mysteries

- ✓ 3-D physical puzzles (like the various metal puzzles available)

- ✓ Mathematic equations

- ✓ Picture puzzles (like *The Clock Without a Face*)

- ✓ Codes and Cyphers (like the infamous Beale Cyphers)

- ✓ Mazes

- ✓ Scrabble

- ✓ Police dramas

Essentially, puzzles increase creativity because they help create new neural pathways and new ways of thinking—different perspectives. They expand your thought processes. Those new perspectives can then aid in helping you "see" differently in a creative process. Where it can get really exciting is when we bring together both the creative and critical thought processes.

Consider this: Very often, the end goal for our business is to supply solutions to our customers' problems. The solutions we provide may help them start something (like a new business), create something (like a book), stop something (like smoking), or avoid something (like being drawn into an unhealthy relationship). Because puzzles force us to see from different perspectives and search for the clues that bring us to the solution, they can also aid us in parallel forms of thinking as well in our businesses. The best way to provide a solution to a puzzle (the customer's problem) is to understand the creation process of the puzzle (why this problem exists).

I'm not saying that completing a book of Sudoku is going to help you create better products for your customers. What I am saying, though, is that, from my experience, puzzle solving can help you think about solutions differently, which is a type of creativity!

WAY **10**

Meditation

Meditation means different things to different people. And while it can have spiritual benefit and connotations, I'm primarily referring to it as a practice of quieting your mind and "listening."

Let me ask you a question: Have you ever tried to sit completely silent with no thoughts or anything entering your mind for five minutes? Five minutes doesn't sound like a long period of time, but if you are undisciplined and trying to quiet your mind, it can seem like an eternity. Chances are you wouldn't last more than a few seconds before nagging thoughts began to creep in.

Silence is a very powerful way of tapping into creativity because you are de-cluttering your mind. You're clearing away the hindrances that can cause creativity to stop flowing. With the information overload we often experience nearly every moment of our lives, achieving a few moments of focused silence can be a welcome experience, as well as very beneficial for your creative process.

Try this: Find a quiet place away from interruption. Sitting in a relaxed position and with eyes closed, focus on your breath going in and out. When your mind begins to wander, and it will, bring your focus back to your breath. In time, you will feel yourself relax and find the process easier and more productive.

Prayer is another for of meditation that I've used quite often. It doesn't have to be a set prayer, or even a prayer based on a specific religious doctrine. Prayer is simply communication with a higher power, with the Divine.

I worked for years as a graphic designer and designed nearly 600 book covers over the course of my career. Even to this day, when working on a new project or design, I will pray, "Will you please reveal an inspired design that perfectly complements this project? Thank you!" Then I'm still and listen for ideas. Many times, design ideas will pop into my head in complete form.

Meditation works in the same way that many of the methods shared in this book do, it helps create an environment within your mind that allows a greater flow of creativity. Creativity flows, and meditation is one of the best methods I've found to increase it. As a matter of fact, meditation is something I do every night. If you peered into my house late at night on any given night, you would find me walking back and forth in my house, pacing and listening. A notepad is always available for ideas and the house is silent. Sometimes I'll ask a question and then "listen" for a response. Other times I will just pace with a clear mind. As a matter of fact, before I wrote each of these 21 Ways, I took time to meditate on each one while pacing around my house. When I felt clear on what I wanted to say, I sat down and wrote on that particular "Way."

The meditation process isn't just a great practice for business ideas; it's an effective method for getting clear in any area of your life. Since each part of your life affects every other part, you'll always benefit from a consistent practice of meditation.

11

Research

When you think about increasing creativity, research probably isn't the first idea that comes to mind. We often associate research with analytical, mind-numbing number crunching and fact checking. While it can be that, research can also take on a much more fun role.

Research can be a very creative process. I love research. If you haven't figured it out by now, I'm a research-aholic. Whenever you're researching a topic—it can be any topic—it's the journey of the process that provides us with the gift of creativity. Think of it as sensory input for your computer (your brain) to process, make comparisons and connect dots in ways you may not have considered before.

Research opens up the door for curiosity and curiosity leads to creativity.

One of my favorite, creativity-boosting parts of research is following the proverbial "rabbit trails." I'm sure you know what rabbit trails are; it's when you become distracted from your main research topic because something else piques your curiosity. There are times when avoiding rabbit trails at all costs is important to stay on task. But from a creativity perspective, allowing your mind wander by following curiosity can lead to some pretty amazing breakthroughs. Rabbit trails are great places to discover what you never knew existed, and following one "dot" to the next "dot" can lead to an unexpected and wonderful creative journey. So have fun and explore!

Another research method I use to help boost my own creativity is to explore what others are creating in my area of interest, or in related areas. For example, I was recently hired to design a book cover and the author requested a design style that was similar to Andy Warhol's distinct pop art style. I never had designed a book cover in that style before, so I researched what others had designed using that approach. I wasn't looking to copy what they had created. Rather, I was researching to discover what the design guidelines and standards were for that art style so that, when I created my own design, it would resemble that particular motif. The end result turned out great and the customer was pleased.

I use the same research approach when identifying potential niche markets to create products for. I want to see what others are creating in that market. Often I will purchase a number of the products, not to copy what they are doing, but to identify the solutions people are looking for and to identify possible unaddressed areas that I can fill or expand upon. This approach to product creation has been one of the most profitable, creative approaches I've discovered. Research what exists. Identify holes. Fill the holes. That way, you no longer compete with the other products; you complement them!

12

Idea Mashing

Idea mashing is when you take two or more seemingly unrelated ideas and "mash" them together to form something new. The premise of this creativity booster is, "I wonder what would happen if we mixed it up *this* way?"

You often see "idea mashing" explored in foods. Bacon ice cream, Vanilla Coke, peanut and pickle sandwiches (a personal favorite), and other interesting and sometimes bizarre combinations can result in new hit food ideas! Some of today's most popular and unusual recipes began with someone wondering how a new mashup of foods would taste.

The same idea mashing approach is being used in book publishing. Referred to as mash-ups, authors are taking literary standards from the Public Domain and adding new, bizarre elements to the story lines. In one example, *Pride and Prejudice* by Jane Austen, zombies were added to the mix, with the resulting mash up, *Pride and Prejudice and Zombies*, a huge success. Other popular new book mashups include, *Abraham Lincoln, Vampire Killer* and *Sense and Sensibility and Sea Monsters*.

A common response to the concept of idea mashing is that "you can't do it *that* way." "That isn't the way it's done." This is of course precisely why you *should* experiment. Idea mashing is a beautiful creativity tool that allows you to question everything because it encourages you to see the end result from new perspectives and possibilities. That's a good thing! Consider this question: What would happen if you did everything your industry or market told you *not* to do? Would you create a brand-new market that could explode with sales? Would you create the next big trend? The smartphone and tablet craze is a perfect example of the awesome potential of idea mashing. Think about it, somewhere in the not-so-distant past, someone wondered, "I wonder what would happen if a cell phone could be *more* that just a phone?"

Idea mashing can be applied to any market, product or service. As a matter of fact, I would strongly encourage you to consider this approach. Many breakthroughs in different fields of study were the result of idea mashing—someone wondering what would happen if you mixed this with that. Why not begin asking those same questions about your products, services, and market? Who knows, you may just invent the "next big thing!"

13

Visualization

Close your eyes and clear your mind of all the distractions of the day. Now imagine yourself logging into your merchant account. You smile big because the balance hasn't dipped below $15,000 in months.

Think about the buzz your latest product is creating and the dozens of testimonials you have received from customers thanking you for helping them achieve their own success.

In your mind's eye, you look out the window from your office. In the driveway sits your dream car. You've waited a long time to own one, and now you've been able to realize that dream and pay cash! Enjoy the feeling of satisfaction and accomplishment knowing that this was not a one-time accident, but a deliberate plan you can replicate over and over again.

Imagine pondering what's next for your business. See yourself talking on the phone with the top leaders in your industry and they are sharing what your next steps should be. You're grateful for their advice because it has always proven profitable for you. As you hang up the phone in this visualization, see yourself writing down the strategies your mentor shared. You know this is the answer you've been looking for to take your business to the next level. As you pick up the note pad, look intently at what you wrote down. What does it say?

Visualization is a powerful creative tool you can use to access incredible insights, skills, and abilities. It's so powerful, in fact, that it is a regular part of the training regimen of most professional athletes and Olympic contenders, NASA astronauts and highly successful corporate CEOs. Its benefits are also discussed in detail in the highly regarded success classic, *Think and Grow Rich* by Napoleon Hill.

For example, a basketball player might sit down, close his eyes, and in his mind imagine himself shooting foul shots over and over again. He sees himself taking the stance and focusing on the basket. He feels the ball leave his fingertips as he releases the shot. He watches the ball go through the hoop perfectly and then he sees himself doing it all over again. He may go through this exercise hundreds, if not thousands, of times. Speaking of basketball, even Michael Jordan attributes some of his success to the power of visualization.

Visualization is a creative tool I use all the time. Just as in the example I shared at the beginning of this section, I see myself creating products, checking email, logging into my PayPal account to see the latest total (which is whatever I want it to be). I see the sales come in. I see the testimonials come in from happy customers. I go through the entire process. I do it every week or every day when I need it. I've noticed that as I have consistently gone through the visualization process my business has improved for the better.

My sales have increased. I have become more calm and relaxed. I've been more creative and gotten a lot more work done. Visualization has been a very valuable creative asset for me in my business.

Of course, visualization is just one part of the creative process. Taking inspired action based on your "mind movies" helps bring those creative images to life. So let me ask you, what kind of life do YOU want to create? Sit down, close your eyes, and begin to create it right now.

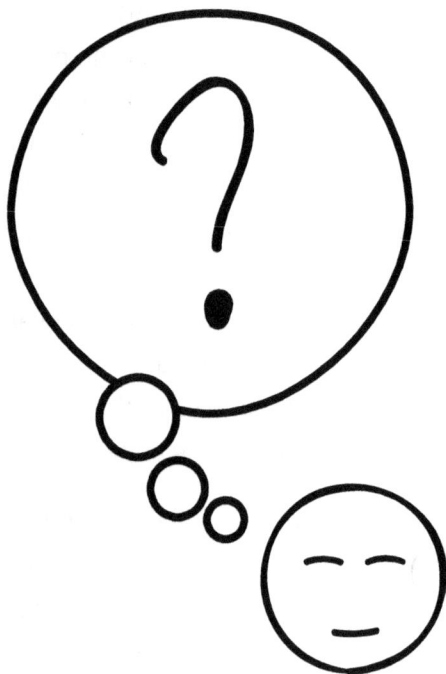

14

Dreaming

Everybody dreams. I'm not one to remember a lot of my dreams, but some of the best ideas that I've "discovered" for my business came either through dreams or as I woke from a dream.

A few years back, I had a dream in which I was talking with Dr. Joe Vitale. In the dream, I asked Joe if there were any new ideas he could share with me concerning the use of public domain content. One of the ideas Joe shared with me was to look at other languages and translations using Wikipedia as a translation source. Then, based on what I discovered on Wikipedia, I should use Google's translator to find public domain content in those other languages.

After waking, I tried what Joe told me to do in the dream and it worked perfectly and became a great research strategy for me for finding foreign language works in the public domain.

Albert Einstein, Paul McCartney, Robert Louis Stevenson, Orson Welles, Thomas Edison, Jack Nicklaus, Stephen King, and many others attribute successes in their lives to dreams.

Another form of dreaming that can prove to be extremely productive from a creative perspective is lucid dreaming. Lucid dreaming is the ability to consciously direct and control your dreams. In a lucid dream, your inner dream world transforms into a kind of interactive alternate reality. Everything you see, hear, feel, taste, and even smell seems as authentic as the waking world.

I know from my own experience that lucid dreams certainly appear more real than an average dream you have at night. I've been able to make conscious decisions during a lucid dream, ask questions, and interact with the people and places I've seen during those experiences.

One such lucid dream that comes to mind involved a book cover I was hired to design. I was trying to come up with a catchy design for the book, but I'd met with little success. I put my head down on the desk and closed my eyes. Suddenly, in my dream I was in a gigantic library. I somehow knew that this library contained a copy of every book ever written. I saw a librarian nearby so I walked over to her and asked if she could show me where I could find a copy of the book I was working on. She took me to the correct section and I pulled the book off the shelf to see what design was on the cover. As soon as I saw the design, I lifted my head and created the exact design on my computer. That book now has the cover design I saw in that library.

While space will not allow me to discuss the methods of enhancing your dreams or lucid dreaming, what I can share is how important it is to keep a journal by your bed. The moment you wake, write down your dreams. Don't think that a dream was so amazing that you could never forget it. More times than not, you will. Write them down, and if your dreams reveal an idea or answer to take action on, do it!

Something else to test (I do this all the time): Give your subconscious homework for while you sleep.

Before you doze off, say, "Okay subconscious, I need ideas for this problem. Work through scenarios while I sleep, and let me know what you come up with when I wake up." Many times I have awakened to some pretty awesome ideas using that method.

WAY 15

Role-Playing

Have you ever watched a crime drama on television where the detectives will role-play their idea of how a crime went down to see if they can gain new insights? Role-playing can serve as a terrific vehicle for creative inspiration. The reason it can work so effectively is that role-playing offers you a different perspective, a different point of view from what you've already experienced.

You may remember that earlier in the book (in "Way 8: Culture Shifting"), I talked about asking the question, "What would _____ (your favorite mentor) do?" Role-playing works very similarly, except that, instead of asking the question, you actually play out the role. I stumbled into the power of role-playing quite by accident when I was on my first newspaper photo assignment.

My first assignment as a newspaper photographer was to take pictures at a local college where an Army general was being honored. At age 19, I was very shy and quiet, so the idea of telling Army generals where to stand and how to pose had me seriously stressed out. I was noticeably shaking. Something happened when I walked in the door to the event, however. The even organizer saw me walk in with my camera and declared, "Oh good, the photographer is here from the paper." When I heard her say that, something happened to me. I was no longer Tony, the shy teenager; I was "the photographer."

Photographers do photographer "stuff," such as tell people where to stand and how to pose, and in that moment, I assumed that role completely. I felt confident and in charge and got the photos and information I needed for the story with no problems. It was cool, actually. Of course, after the assignment was over and I was "Tony" again, I sat in my dad's truck and shook with disbelief at what I had just done. Over time, I realized that I had that confidence in me all along and, while shy Tony is still a part of who I am, I was able to adopt this newfound confidence as another aspect of my personality.

In business, if you want to do affiliate sales or create products maybe you don't want to ask how someone would do it. You might want to take on the role of somebody who's already done it.

One of the easiest ways to enjoy the benefits of role-playing is to establish a new character using a pen name. Many writers and actors use a pen name or a stage or screen name as a part of a new "role." You can experiment and view results from a completely new perspective using role-playing. I have a number of pen names, including a few female ones. When creating them, I am as complete as I can be in establishing whom each one is as a person, including name, hometown, hobbies, and interests. It enables me to get into that character more completely, which enhances the creative process. Try it; you'll be amazed by the experience!

WAY 16

Point of View

As a photographer and photography teacher, one of the primary lessons I covey to my students is the importance of point of view. I've found that most people when taking a photograph will point the camera and the subject and snap the photo straight on. While this approach can make sense at times, there are so many other creative possibilities available to you if you simply change your point of view.

Let's say you see a tree standing alone in the middle of a field and you want to take a photo of it. From where you are standing, you pull out your camera (it doesn't matter what type), center the tree in your viewfinder or on the LCD screen, and snap the photo. Congratulations! You now have a photo of a tree. But, what would happen if you changed the perspective of your photo? What if you took a photo of the tree:

✓ Standing closer

✓ With a child playing in its leaves

✓ Standing 100 feet farther to the left or right

✓ Lying on the ground under the tree and shooting up

✓ Using a macro lens to get up really close to its leaves

✓ Using a wide angle or telephoto lens

✓ At sunrise or sunset

✓ Looking down on it from a helicopter

✓ As a long exposure at night

✓ In all four seasons

These are just a few examples of different points of view you could use for one photograph. I could list a lot more. You get the idea. Very often, you can get locked in to doing and seeing things the one particular way. There isn't anything wrong with systems and methods—you need them to give your work consistency and excellence—but when they stifle creativity, you have a problem.

Again, this is one of those processes to help you to think and "see" differently.

Let's consider your business, product or service using this creativity booster of point of view. How is your product or service perceived from the perspective of:

- ✓ A soccer mom?

- ✓ An unemployed, college educated Asian male?

- ✓ A retired veteran?

- ✓ A 13-year-old girl?

- ✓ A young family about to lose a home to foreclosure?

- ✓ A middle-aged non–English-speaking woman living in Brazil?

- ✓ A highly successful CEO?

In the global economy we do business in today, these individuals, and countless others, interact with your business, product, or service, bringing unique points of view. If you can understand that and adapt your business where it makes sense to do so, you can increase your sales and the effectiveness of your product or service. Or, you can just go on viewing your business from the same perspective. You have a choice and making change can be hard or scary. But I believe the results are worth it.

A first step is looking into who your audience is. An easy way to gain some insight is to go to Quantcast.com and type in the URL of your website, as well as those of your competitors. Quantcast will show you your target demographic based on current visitors accessing the websites. Using that data, consider how you can better serve their points of view.

Resources in this Way:

 Quantcast.com

17

Self-Expression

Because we are creative beings, self-expression is vital to our existence and is a key to explosive creativity. Self-expression takes diverse forms, but at its core it is our ability to express who we are as creative beings by doing the things we love. That expression may take on the form of:

- ✓ Dance
- ✓ Photography
- ✓ Crafts
- ✓ Walking
- ✓ Hunting
- ✓ Singing

✓ Painting

✓ Building bird feeders

✓ Gardening

✓ Writing

The possibilities for self-expression are as diverse as the people who populate our planet. Why is self-expression so important to increasing the creativity in our lives? Simple. It's easy to get trapped in the mundane experience of living life. Busyness, necessary or invented, can shut down our creative processes and demote us to where we are little more than drone worker bees, doing the same things day in and day out.

Expressing ourselves through any creative outlet allows us to tap into the "stuff" that makes us unique. It's what we often do to relax. And when we do tap into our creative sides, something interesting begins to take place. Because we are "priming our creative pump," the creative flow can carry over into other areas our lives as well. In other words, when we embrace creativity in one area of our life, it becomes contagious and spreads into other areas of our lives as well.

Self-expression also affects us physiologically. Because we are often in a state of bliss while enjoying our expressive activity, positive endorphins are released into our body that create an ongoing sense of well being. Do you think that will affect other areas of your life, such as your business? You bet it will!

There is another way I'd like you to consider self-expression as well. The exercise borrows from "Way 16: Point of View." It's likely you have seen or heard an aspect of this concept before. Consider the following questions:

✓ If I were a dance, how would I move, and why?

✓ If I were a song, what would it sound like, and why?

✓ If I were an animal, why kind of animal would I be, and why?

✓ If I were a plant, what type of plant would I be, and why?

✓ If I were a color, what color would I be, and why?

Considering these questions as a form of self-expression can lead you to some very curious discoveries about yourself. The answers may also reveal some areas of creativity in your life that you never considered before. I encourage you to pon-der each of the questions listed above and allow them to paint images and sounds on the screen of your mind (Way 13: Visualization).

Allow the experience to take on a life of its own and just observe. I can guarantee that the creative discoveries you make will translate into a renewed appreciation for who you are, as well as a "shot in the arm" for your creative expression.

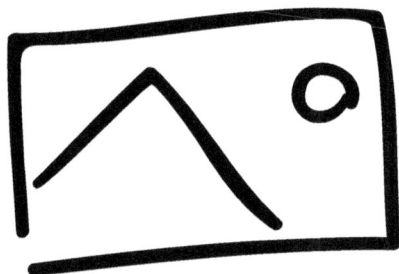

18

Hypnosis

When you are thinking about ways to boost or enhance your creativity, hypnosis is likely not going to be the first method that comes to mind. It probably will not be the second or third either, but hear me out on this one. Hypnosis can be a very powerful creativity booster in a couple of exciting ways.

Hypnosis offers a number of beneficial outcomes that can directly relate to increased creativity. You have likely noticed by now that most, if not all, of the "Ways" shared in this book can be filtered down into two broad categories: Ways that offer a different perspective and Ways that address hindrances to creative flow. Hypnosis would qualify as one of the latter because it can be very effective in removing mental blocks to our thinking.

Some successful hypnotic treatments I have seen as relating to creativity include success over:

✓ A fear of public speaking

✓ Shyness

✓ Lack of confidence

✓ Loss of creative edge

By taking you through a simple, non-invasive hypnotic induction, a skilled hypnotherapist can help you remove blockages that prevent you from enjoying the experiences you wish to embrace. Using empowering language, your hypnotherapist reprograms your consciousness in a positive way that supports your desire for success in a given area. The therapist can never make you do anything that you are unwilling to do; however, the positive benefits can be truly transformational in some cases.

Another area of hypnosis that warrants some examination is the practice of past life regression. While this section is not offered for debate as to the validity of reincarnation, past life regression is worth considering as a creativity booster because of the possible implications behind the achieved results.

During a past life regression hypnosis session, the subject is asked a series of questions to determine information about the past lives she may have experienced. The first time I had this done, I was extremely skeptical because I thought the questions were leading and working with my imagination to create memories that were not real.

What I didn't expect, however, were the emotions that were attached to what I remembered. At times, the emotions were overpowering. It was as if I were actually experiencing or had experienced what I saw. Once the session was over, I could see direct correlations between those memories and who I am as a person today. I've never been able to shake it.

Whether I experienced actual moments from my past lives or just visualized representations of different areas of my psyche, in the end it didn't matter to me. What does matter is that, through that experience of regression, I became more keenly aware of those aspects of my life. That awareness definitely led to increased creativity.

WAY 19

Physical Exercise & Massage Therapy

Before you begin to moan about exercise, hear me out. Believe it or not, there is a lot of great benefit in boosting your creativity through regular physical exercise and massage therapy.

Studies have shown that our muscles tighten and retain toxins due to stress, low water intake, and other issues. These toxins, then, can have a profound effect on your body and mind, causing a lack of sleep, brain fog, achiness, and much more.

As we exercise, we give our body and muscles permission to release the tension and toxins that build up in them. Yes, we are often tired, but we are also more relaxed as well. End your exercise time with an Epson salts soak and you will feel invigorated, like a new person.

Simple, low-impact exercises such as leg bends, stretches, push-ups, and sit-ups done in a regular, consistent manner will not only keep your body's toxins to a minimum, but they will also aid in improving your health overall.

I would also recommend regular visits to a licensed massage therapist. Massage therapy offers similar results, except in a more passive way.

Exercise also signals the release of endorphins, which trigger a positive feeling in the body. You've likely heard of a "runner's high" that comes from jogging. The endorphin rush in your brain causes that high. Endorphins have been shown to affect us in beneficial ways, including:

✓ A positive impact on depression and anxiety

✓ Counteracting of feelings of withdrawal and hopelessness

✓ Reduction of stress

✓ Noticeable reduction of tension, fatigue, and anger

With reduced stress, anxiety, and depression, creativity and imagination will come much more easily, and that's precisely what we are after!

20

Chunking

You have no doubt discovered, at one time in your life or another, how easy it is to make easy tasks extremely difficult. Rather than stick with the famous acronym, KISS (Keep It Simple Stupid), we add on and increase and expand our tasks until they become unwieldy beasts to contend with. Very often, we limit our creativity because we think too big, too complicated. Instead, we should consider simplifying our tasks by "chunking" them.

Chunking breaks down large or complex tasks into manageable pieces, which then frees up creativity to flow more freely because we do not have to "figure it all out" at once. When we take a chunking approach, we can start simple and then develop our idea over time into something more elaborate.

This lesson was brought home to me a few years back during a coaching call with one of my mentors. During our half-hour call, he shared a lot of strategies with me and asked lots of questions about what I was doing in my business.

One of the questions he asked me was whether or not I had a back-end or high-end product to offer my customers? When I told him I was working on one, he asked what I meant by "working." I told him that it takes time to write and put together a quality high-end product, describing the long-term process I was using. He asked, "What the hell are you doing that for? Dude, you're doing it all wrong. You're going about it all wrong."

He then went on to tell me how to bring something usable and solid to market in just a few days by breaking the big task of creating this new product into smaller, more manageable steps. I followed his advice and quickly introduced a product that was a huge success. I've followed his model ever since. His way to handle product creation was easy and simple. He chunked down the process, when I was making it nearly impossible with my multi-step approach.

Take this book for instance. The target word count for this book was 10,000 to 12,000 words. Looking at the task from that perspective can seem pretty intimidating. However, this book is comprised of "21 Ways" that are each around 500 words. Sitting down to write 500 words is much easier than trying to write 12,000 words. Do you get the idea? That's chunking at work.

Chunking can also make it much easier to wrap your brain around huge concepts or numbers. Let's say you wanted to make $1 million this year. If you're like most people, the idea of making a million bucks seems almost impossible. But if you break it down into a manageable amount, suddenly your creativity soars and you immediately believe you can do it.

Here is an example. Let's say you could create a website that sold a product, your own product or an affiliate product, and you made just $100 a day. Not a difficult task. That's two to three sales a day. Out of the millions of people who are online, it's highly likely that you can find two or three people to buy the product. Now here is where the magic is: If you have just twenty-seven of those websites, each making just two to three sales a day, you will earn $1 million in the next twelve months. By itself, a million seems impossible, but twenty-seven is definitely doable!

That's the power of chunking. You could come up with all sorts of complicated, challenging ideas to earn $1 million or complete some other insurmountable task, but break it down to its simplest components and suddenly it's possible. Kind of like the old axiom of how to eat an elephant: one bite at a time!

21

Food and Supplements

The last "Way" to increase creativity I want to look at is through food and supplements. What you eat has a huge effect on how creative you are. Eating a lot of sugar, gluten, and salt will slow your body's metabolism down, causing you to feel lethargic and tired.

These ingredients, found in most junk food and processed foods, can also cause brain fog, and many other anti-creative physiological effects in your body. Sure, you may experience a temporary rush of energy, also known as a sugar high, but before long, you crash and you've bottomed out.

Conversely, eating healthy, whole foods, including a lot of greens, slow-burn carbs, and organic protein-based foods, creates the opposite effect. You have more energy, more focus, and, as a result, more creativity!

I can tell you from experience that, when I switched to an organic, healthy diet, it made a huge difference in my energy levels and my ability to think clearly. A simple meal change, such as eating eggs and black beans for breakfast, increases my metabolism and energy levels to the point where I go through much of the morning feeling almost euphoric.

Other foods that are excellent for improving brain function include avocados, blueberries, wild salmon, nuts, seeds, broccoli, and spinach.

Studies have also shown that including certain supplements, such as Acetyl L-Carnatine, CoQ10, and *Gingko biloba*, can improve brain function. While I'm not a doctor and will encourage you to do your own research on the health benefits of different supplements, I can share my own experience and have found that supplements like these have definitely contributed to increased feelings of alertness and clarity.

When you think about it, it makes sense that, when you eat healthy, your body will respond in positive ways. Unfortunately, many have never realized that their poor diet is contributing to their loss of energy, focus, and creativity!

About the Author

Tony Laidig is a professional photographer, graphic artist, storyteller and recognized specialist at creating information products using all types of media.

Tony's moving, daily photographic exploration, "A Day with the Sacred," has inspired thousands to consider what they consider sacred and why. As a graphic artist, he designed nearly 600 book covers for best-selling authors around the world. And in teaching step-by-step product creation processes, Tony has helped thousands of individuals create new products, and income streams, of their own.

At the heart of Tony's passion for telling stories through these different mediums lies a curious commitment to the creative process and help others connect with the creativity they have within.

FREE BONUS!

If you enjoyed *21 Ways to Skyrocket Your Creativity*, then I have a very special surprise for you. A while back, I taught a special tele seminar series called, *The Creativity Code*. Some of that teaching became the foundation for this book. As a special bonus, I'd like to *give* you free access to those audios! I go a *lot* more in-depth on each of the creativity methods and even share a few more. I also spend some time discussing hindrances to creativity and how to recognize and remove this blockages. I regularly sell *The Creativity Code* for $97, but it's yours FREE!

In fact, here's just a small sampling of what you'll discover during this breakthrough teleseminar series:

- ✓ How to apply creativity and innovation to *any* situation

- ✓ Why being a copycat in your product creation can be the kiss of death to your business

- ✓ How to stop the endless, distractive chatter in your mind

- ✓ What one thing will kill your creativity *every* time

- ✓ How to almost instantly come up with an endless number of business ideas

- ✓ Why the bathroom seems to be the ultimate creativity spot

- ✓ The secrets your dog holds to amazing creativity

- ✓ How to determine which ideas to act on quickly and easily

- ✓ The role your emotions play in the success of your business

- ✓ Why less can be much more

- ✓ How to easily gain quick access to any guru or mentor

- ✓ Why the Public Domain is one of the best enhancers of creativity

- ✓ How to identify with laser-focused accuracy the actions that keep you from success

- ✓ Why creativity plus action will make you unstoppable

- ✓ And much, much more!

You can access *The Creativity Code* audios by simply visiting the page below. Enter your name and e-mail address, and you'll receive instant access!

ProvenContent.com/creativitycode

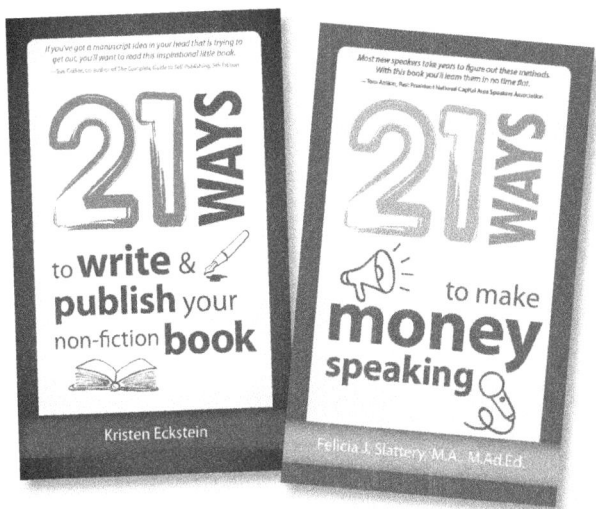

Don't miss a single book in the series!

Look for more *21 Ways*™ books at:

21WaysBooks.com

www.ingramcontent.com/pod-product-compliance
Lightning Source LLC
Chambersburg PA
CBHW071240020426
42333CB00015B/1566